United States Government Accountability Office

Testimony
Before the Special Committee on
Aging, U.S. Senate

I0410866

For Release on Delivery
Expected at 2:15 p.m. ET
Wednesday, September 10, 2014

OLDER AMERICANS

Inability to Repay Student Loans May Affect Financial Security of a Small Percentage of Retirees

Statement of Charles A. Jeszeck, Director, Education, Workforce, and Income Security

GAO-14-866T

OLDER AMERICANS

Inability to Repay Student Loans May Affect Financial Security of a Small Percentage of Retirees

GAO Highlights

Highlights of GAO-14-866T, a testimony before the Special Committee on Aging, U.S. Senate

Why GAO Did This Study

Recent studies have indicated that many Americans may be approaching their retirement years with increasing levels of various kinds of debt. Such debt can reduce net worth and income, thereby diminishing overall retirement financial security. Student loan debt held by older Americans can be especially daunting because unlike other types of debt, it generally cannot be discharged in bankruptcy. GAO was asked to examine the extent of student loan debt held by older Americans and the implications of default.

This testimony provides information on: (1) the extent to which older Americans have outstanding student loans and how this debt compares to other types of debt, and (2) the extent to which older Americans have defaulted on federal student loans and the possible consequences of default. To address these issues, GAO obtained and analyzed relevant data from the Federal Reserve Board's Survey of Consumer Finances as well as data from the Department of the Treasury, the Social Security Administration, and the Department of Education. GAO also reviewed key agency documents and interviewed knowledgeable staff.

What GAO Recommends

GAO is not making recommendations. GAO received technical comments on a draft of this testimony from the Department of Education, the Department of the Treasury, and the Federal Reserve System. GAO incorporated these comments into the testimony as appropriate.

View GAO-14-866T. For more information, contact Charles A. Jeszeck at (202) 512-7215 or jeszeckc@gao.gov.

What GAO Found

Comparatively few households headed by older Americans carry student debt compared to other types of debt, such as for mortgages and credit cards. GAO's analysis of the data from the Survey of Consumer Finances reveals that about 3 percent of households headed by those aged 65 or older—about 706,000 households—carry student loan debt. This compares to about 24 percent of households headed by those aged 64 or younger—22 million households. Compared to student loan debt, those 65 and older are much more likely to carry other types of debt. For example, about 29 percent carry home mortgage debt and 27 percent carry credit card debt. Still, student debt among older American households has grown in recent years. The percentage of households headed by those aged 65 to 74 having student debt grew from about 1 percent in 2004 to about 4 percent in 2010. While those 65 and older account for a small fraction of the total amount of outstanding federal student debt, the outstanding federal student debt for this age group grew from about $2.8 billion in 2005 to about $18.2 billion in 2013.

Outstanding Federal Student Loan Balances by Age Group, 2005 and 2013

Source: GAO analysis of data provided by the Department of Education. | GAO-14-866T

Available data indicate that borrowers 65 and older hold defaulted federal student loans at a much higher rate, which can leave some retirees with income below the poverty threshold. Although federal student loans can remain unpaid for more than a year before the Department of Education takes aggressive action to recover the funds, once initiated, the actions can have serious consequences. For example, a portion of the borrower's Social Security disability, retirement, or survivor benefits can be claimed to pay off the loan. From 2002 through 2013, the number of individuals whose Social Security benefits were offset to pay student loan debt increased about five-fold from about 31,000 to 155,000. Among those 65 and older, the number of individuals whose benefits were offset grew from about 6,000 to about 36,000 over the same period, roughly a 500 percent increase. In 1998, additional limits on the amount that monthly benefits can be offset were implemented, but since that time the value of the amount protected and retained by the borrower has fallen below the poverty threshold.

_____ United States Government Accountability Office

Chairman Nelson, Ranking Member Collins, and Members of the Committee:

I am pleased to be here today to discuss the financial effect of student loan debt on older Americans.[1] This statement summarizes the work we did at the request of Chairman Nelson and Chairman Harkin, Chair of the Senate Committee on Health, Education, Labor, and Pensions. As recent studies have shown, debt held by older Americans is increasing and may affect financial security in retirement. A 2013 study reported that the percentage of Americans 65 or older with some debt increased from about 30 percent to about 43 percent from 1998 to 2010.[2] The study also found that the median amount of debt increased 56 percent, from about $13,600 to $21,200. Further, for those 65 and older, the overall debt ratio—total debt as a percentage of total household assets—doubled from 1998 to 2010, rising from 6.4 percent to 13 percent. Such debt reduces net worth and income and can erode retirement security. The effect of rising debt can be more profound for those who have accumulated few or no financial assets.

Student loan debt can be especially problematic because unlike other types of debt, it generally cannot be discharged in bankruptcy[3] and can, in the event of default on federal student loans, lead to reductions in certain federal payments such as Social Security benefits.[4] According to data compiled by the Federal Reserve Bank of New York, the number of Americans 50 and older with student loan debt increased from 3 million in 2005 to 6.9 million in 2012—an increase of 130 percent.

In light of these issues, we were asked to examine both the incidence of student loan debt among older American households, and the implications of defaulting on student loans for members of this population. Specifically, we examined (1) the extent to which older Americans have

---

[1] In this testimony, we use the phrase "older Americans" to mean those of traditional retirement age, 65 and older. As appropriate, we will also consider those approaching retirement age which, depending on the data source, may include those at or over the ages of 50 or 55.

[2] Nadia Karamcheva, *Is Household Debt Growing for Older Americans?* Urban Institute Program on Retirement Policy, Number 33, (January 2013).

[3] 11 U.S. C. § 523(a)(8).

[4] 31 U.S.C. § 3716(c)(3)(A)(i)(I).

outstanding student loans and how this debt compared to other types of debt, and (2) the extent to which older Americans have defaulted on federal student loans and the possible consequences of default.

To address these questions, we analyzed a number of nationally representative datasets, reviewed relevant literature, examined relevant federal laws and regulations, studied agency data and documents, and interviewed relevant experts. Specifically, for the first question, we extracted and analyzed data from the Federal Reserve Board's Survey of Consumer Finances (SCF), a survey conducted once every 3 years that gathers various economic and financial data at the household level. We also obtained targeted data reflecting individual loans—but not borrowers—from the Department of Education's (Education) National Student Loan Data System (NSLDS). Although Education maintains borrower-level data, it was only able to provide us with aggregated data by loan type during the course of our analyses. To answer the second question, we reviewed additional data from the NSLDS, and obtained data from the Department of the Treasury (Treasury) on payments withheld from Social Security benefits and applied to defaulted federal student loans through the Treasury Offset Program. To better understand offset for older Americans, we matched the Treasury data with data from the Social Security Administration's Master Beneficiary Record on the ages of these borrowers and the types of benefits they receive. In addition, we interviewed Education officials and reviewed relevant documentation regarding Education's debt collection policies and procedures; however, we did not audit their compliance with statutory requirements related to these activities. We assessed the reliability of the data sources by reviewing documentation and conducting testing of the data and determined that they were sufficiently reliable for purposes of this testimony. More details on our scope and methodology are included in appendix 1.

We provided a draft of this testimony to the Department of Education, the Department of the Treasury, the Social Security Administration, and the Federal Reserve System for review and comment. They generally agreed with our findings. We received technical comments from each agency except the Social Security Administration, which had no comments, and as appropriate, we incorporated these technical comments into this testimony.

We conducted this performance audit from November 2013 to September 2014 in accordance with generally accepted government auditing standards. Those standards require that we plan and perform the audit to obtain sufficient, appropriate evidence to provide a reasonable basis for our findings and conclusions based on our audit objectives. We believe that the evidence obtained provides a reasonable basis for our findings and conclusions based on our audit objectives.

Background

Since passage of the Higher Education Act of 1965,[5] a broad array of federal student aid programs, including loan programs, have been available to help students finance the cost of postsecondary education.[6] Currently, several types of federal student loans administered by Education make up the largest portion of student loans in the United States. Four types of federal student loans are available to borrowers and have features that make them attractive for financing higher education. For example, borrowers are not required to begin repaying most federal student loans until after graduation or when their enrollment status significantly changes. Further, interest rates on federal student loans are generally lower than other financing alternatives, and the programs offer repayment flexibilities if borrowers are unable to meet scheduled payments. As outlined in table 1, the four federal loan programs differ in that interest rates may or may not be subsidized based on the borrower's financial need, loans may be designed to specifically serve undergraduate or graduate and professional students, and loans may serve to consolidate and extend the payment term of multiple federal student loans.[7]

[5]Pub. L. No. 89-329, 79 Stat. 1219 (codified as amended at 20 U.S.C. §§ 1001-1161aa-1 and 42 U.S.C. §§ 2751-2757b).

[6]In addition to loans, the Higher Education Act of 1965 also authorizes various other types of federal support for higher education, including grants and scholarships.

[7]In addition to the loan programs described in table 1, many older borrowers may be carrying Federal Family Education Loans (FFEL). The FFEL program was authorized by the Higher Education Act of 1965, but the SAFRA Act terminated the authority to make FFEL loans after June 30, 2010 (Pub. L. No. 111-152, §§ 2001 and 2201, 124 Stat. 1029, 1071 and 1074 (codified at 20 U.S.C. § 1071(b) and (d)) and no additional loans have been made.

Table 1: Major Types of Federal Student Loans

Federal loan program	Eligibility	Aggregate loan limits	Interest rates[a]
Federal Perkins Loans	Undergraduate and graduate students who can demonstrate financial need	$11,000 for 1st and 2nd year undergraduate students $27,500 for 3rd and 4th year undergraduate students $60,000 for graduate students (including undergraduate loans)	5%
William D. Ford Direct Stafford Loans	Subsidized loans[b] Undergraduate students enrolled at least half-time who can demonstrate financial need Unsubsidized loans Undergraduate and graduate students. Same as subsidized loans, except financial need is not required	Subsidized $23,000 for undergraduate students $65,000 for graduate students Total (subsidized and unsubsidized) $31,000 for dependent undergraduates $57,500 for independent undergraduates and dependent students whose parents cannot get PLUS loans $138,500 for graduate and professional students	4.66% for undergraduates (subsidized and unsubsidized) 6.21% for graduate and professional (unsubsidized only)
Direct PLUS Loans	Graduate and professional students and parents of dependent undergraduate students Students must be enrolled at least half-time, and applicant must have no adverse credit history Financial need is not required	No aggregate limit	7.21%
Direct Consolidation Loans	Students or parent borrowers wanting to combine multiple federal loans into one loan Parent PLUS loans cannot be transferred to the student and become the student's responsibility	Not applicable	Rate is based on the weighted average of the interest rates of the loans being consolidated, rounded up to the nearest 1/8 of 1%

Source: U.S. Department of Education. | GAO-14-866T

[a]Federal student loan interest rates vary annually based on interest rates available in the financial markets and are determined each spring for new loans being made for the upcoming July 1 through June 30 period. Loans have a fixed interest rate for the life of the loan. The rates in this column apply to loans made on or after July 1, 2014 and before July 1, 2015, excepting Perkins loans, which have an interest rate of 5 percent regardless of the date the loan was disbursed.

[b]Subsidized loans are loans on which the federal government generally pays interest while the student is in school and during certain other periods. In the case of unsubsidized loans, interest starts accruing as soon as funds are disbursed, and the borrower is responsible for paying the interest. Federal Perkins Loans are subsidized as well, but Direct PLUS Loans are not. Direct Consolidation Loans may have both subsidized and unsubsidized components, depending on the loan types that were consolidated.

Education administers federal student loans and is generally responsible for, among other duties, disbursing, reconciling, and accounting for student loans and other student aid, and tracking loan repayment. Although no other federal agencies have a direct role in administering student loans, other agencies may become involved in the event that a borrower fails to make repayment. For example, Education may coordinate with Treasury to withhold a portion of federal payments to borrowers who have not made scheduled loan repayments. Such payment withholding, known as administrative offset, can affect payments to individuals by various federal agencies. Offsets of income tax refunds would involve the Internal Revenue Service and offsets of Social Security retirement or disability benefits would involve the Social Security Administration.

Student loans are also available from private lenders, such as banks and credit unions. Private loans differ from federal loans in that they may require repayment to begin while the student is still in school, they generally have higher interest rates, and the rates may be variable as opposed to fixed. Unlike federal student loans, private student loans may be more difficult to obtain for some potential borrowers because they may require an established credit record and the cost of the loan may depend on the borrower's credit score. Private student loans are a relatively small part of the student loan market, accounting for 10 to 15 percent of outstanding student loan debt—about $150 billion—as of January 2012.

Older Americans—that is, Americans in or approaching retirement—may hold student loans for a number of reasons. For example, because such loans may have a 10- to 25-year repayment horizon, older Americans may still be paying off student loan debt that they accrued when they were much younger. They may also have accrued student loan debt in the course of mid- or late-career re-training and education. In addition, they may be holding loans taken out for the education of their children, either through co-signing or through Parent PLUS loans.

Relatively Few Households Headed by Individuals 65 and Over Hold Student Loan Debt, but the Amount They Owe May Be Significant

According to the 2010 SCF, households headed by older individuals are much less likely than those headed by younger individuals to hold student loan debt.[8] As of 2010, about 3 percent of surveyed households headed by people 65 and older—representing approximately 706,000 households—reported some student loan debt. This compares to 24 percent for households headed by those under 65—representing about 22 million households.[9] The decrease in the incidence of student loan debt is even more marked for households headed by the oldest individuals—only 1 percent of those aged 75 or over reported such debt. Although few older Americans have student debt, a majority of households headed by those 65 and older reported having some kind of debt, most commonly home mortgage debt, followed by credit card and vehicle debt. While the incidence of all debt types declines for households headed by those 65 and over, the incidence of student loan debt declines at a much faster rate. For example, the incidence of student loan debt for the 65-74 age group is less than half of that for the 55-64 age group—4 percent compared to 9 percent. In contrast, the incidence of any type of debt for the older age group is only about 17 percent less than the younger age group—65 percent compared to 78 percent.

---

[8]The 2010 SCF did not use the phrase "student loans", but rather asked respondents whether they have loans for educational expenses. However, for consistency in usage, we will use the phrases "student loans" or "student loan debt" throughout this report. Because of the inclusive wording of the question, the SCF data reflect both federal and private loans.

[9]SCF survey responses are based on the financial situation of an entire household, not just the head of household. Because of this, it is possible that for some households headed by older Americans, the reported student loan debt is held by children or other dependents that are still members of the household.

Table 2: Incidence of Debt by Age of Head of Household and Type of Debt, 2010

Age of head of household	Mortgage[a]	Credit card	Student	Vehicle	Other debt[b]	Any debt
18-34	34%	39%	40%	32%	23%	78%
35-44	57	46	26	41	32	86
45-54	59	46	18	36	35	84
55-64	51	41	9	28	34	78
Total, 18-64	50	43	24	34	31	81
65-74	37	32	4	23	23	65
75 and older	21	22	1	8	13	39
Total, 65 and older	29	27	3	16	18	52
Total, all ages	45	39	19	30	18	75

Source: GAO analysis of Federal Reserve Survey of Consumer Finance SCF 2010 data. | GAO-14-866T

Note: In all cases, the percentages in this table have margins of error of plus or minus 4 percentage points or less, and in the large majority of cases about 2.8 percentage points or less.

[a]Data in this column reflect home mortgage debt other than home equity lines of credit.

[b]Other debt includes home equity lines of credit, other lines of credit, residential debt not for primary residence, installment loans for other than vehicles and education, as well as other types of debt such as loans against pensions or life insurance.

While relatively few older Americans have student debt, data from the SCF suggest that the size of such debt among older Americans may be comparable to that of younger age groups. Among all age groups, the median balances of student and other types of debt are dwarfed by median balances of home mortgage debt. Estimates of median student debt balances for the various age groups range from about $11,400 to about $15,500. Median mortgage debt, in contrast, ranges from about $58,000 to $136,000 among the same groups. Among households headed by those 65 and older, the estimated median student debt was about $12,000, and among those 64 and younger, about $13,000. However, given the small number of older households with student loans, it is important to note that the estimate of student debt for the 65 and older age category is a general approximation.[10]

---

[10]The estimated median student debt of the 65 and older category—about $11,800— carries a statistical margin of error of about $5,800. This occurs because few households in this age group reported student loan debt, and because of the wide dispersion in the outstanding balance figures reported. Because the dollar values for this age group are measured relatively imprecisely, we cannot say that the dollar values were statistically less than $17,500 or greater than $6,000.

From 2004 to 2010, an increasing percentage of households in all SCF age groups have taken on student loan debt (see fig. 1). During the same period, the percentage of households headed by individuals 65 to 74 who had some student loan debt increased from just under 1 percent in 2004 to about 4 percent in 2010—more than a four-fold increase. The percentage of households having student loan debt in the two youngest age household categories—those 18 to 34 and those 35 to 44—were and remain much larger. Their rate of increase in that type of debt from 2004 to 2010 was comparatively modest—about 40 percent and 80 percent, respectively.

Figure 1: Percentage of Families with Student Loans

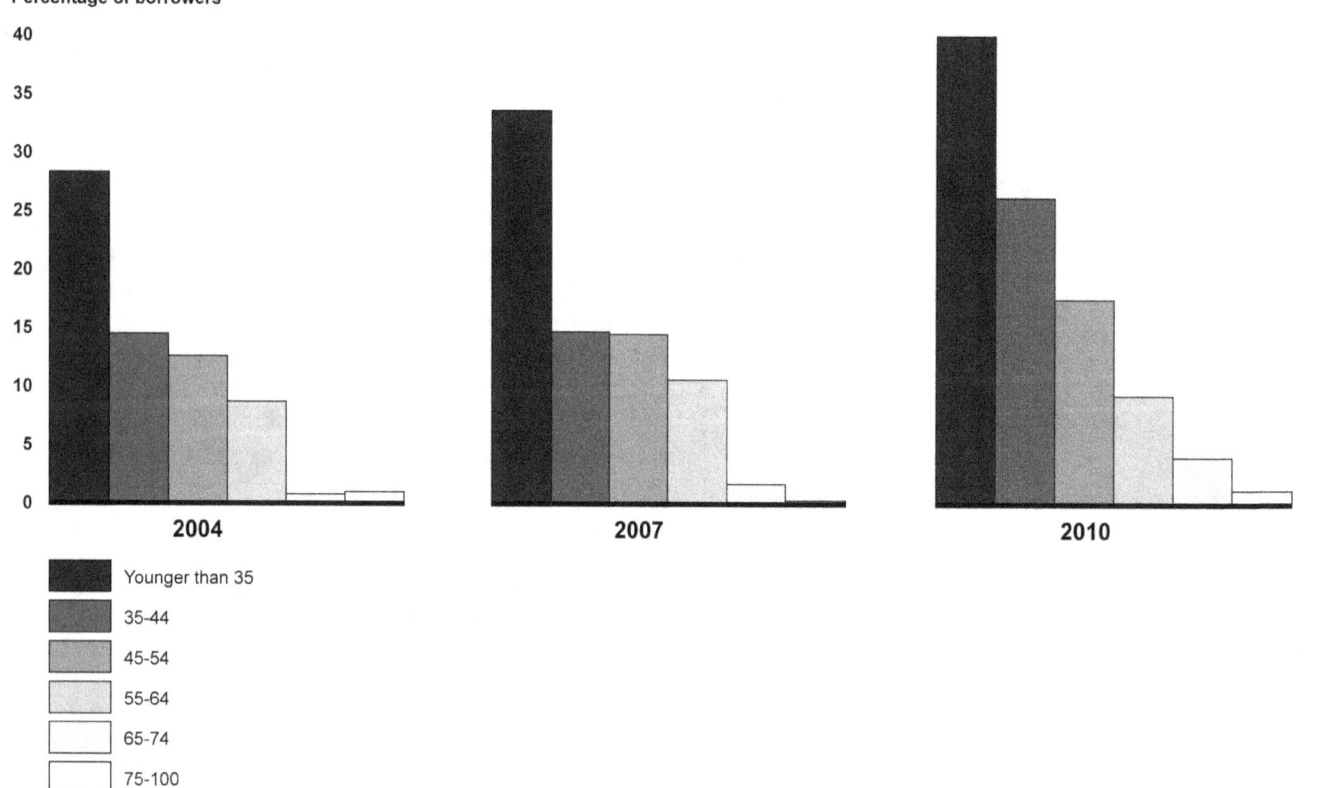

Source: GAO analysis of Survey of Consumer Finances data. | GAO-14-866T

Note: Based on standard errors estimated using the SCF replicate weights, all estimates have a margin of error of 2.4 percentage points or less.

Data from Education's NSLDS also indicates substantial growth in aggregate federal student loan balances among individuals in all age groups, especially older Americans.[11] Aggregate federal student loan debt levels more than doubled overall, rising from slightly more than $400 billion in 2005 to more than $1 trillion dollars in 2013 (see fig. 2). The total outstanding student debt for those 65 and older was and remains a small fraction of total outstanding federal student debt. However, debt for this age group grew at a much faster pace—from about $2.8 billion in 2005 to about $18.2 billion in 2013, more than a six-fold increase.

[11]Data in this paragraph and in figure 3 are drawn from the NSLDS, a comprehensive national database containing information about the federal financial aid history of students receiving federal assistance under Title IV of the Higher Education Act of 1965 (20 U.S.C. §§ 1070-1099d and 42 U.S.C. §§ 2751-2757b). For this reason, it is not perfectly comparable to the SCF, which collects data via survey at the household level, and reflects both federal and private loans as well as other forms of debt. See additional detail about these two data sources in Appendix I.

GAO-14-866T

Figure 2: Outstanding Federal Student Loan Balances by Age Group from Fiscal Years 2005 to 2013

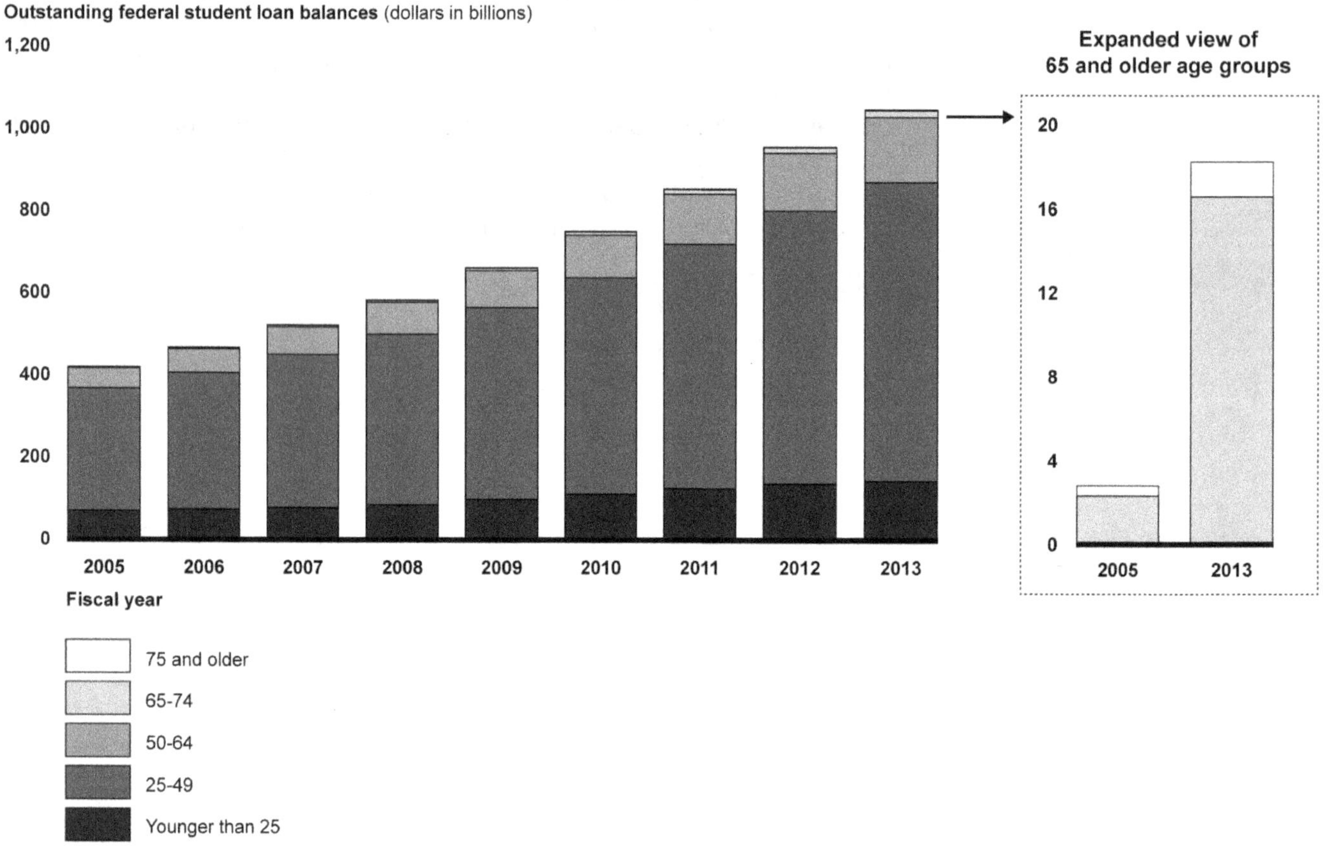

Outstanding federal student loan balances (dollars in billions)

Expanded view of 65 and older age groups

Legend:
- 75 and older
- 65-74
- 50-64
- 25-49
- Younger than 25

Source: GAO analysis of data provided by the Department of Education. | GAO-14-866T

Note: Values have not been corrected for inflation. From 2005 to 2013, prices increased by approximately 23 percent, according to the consumer price index.

Although the Direct PLUS Loan program offers parents of dependent undergraduate students the opportunity to borrow to finance their children's education, data from Education suggests that most federal student loan debt held by older Americans was not incurred on behalf of dependents, but primarily for their own education.[12] About 27 percent of

---

[12]PLUS loans are a form of Direct Loan that can be used by graduate or professional degree students or parents of dependent undergraduate students to pay for educational expenses not paid for by other assistance. 20 U.S.C. § 1078-2. Parents or step-parents are eligible for such loans if their child is a dependent student enrolled at least half-time and the school participates in the Direct Loan Program.

GAO-14-866T

loan balances held by the 50 to 64 age group was for their children, while about 73 percent was for the borrower's own education (see fig. 3). For age groups 65 and over, the percentages of outstanding loan balances attributable to the borrowers' own education are even higher. For those aged 65-74, 82 percent of the outstanding student loan balances was for the individual's own education, and for the 75 and older group, this was true of 83 percent. Because information on the age of the loans was not readily available to us, we do not know the extent to which the debt of older Americans is attributable to recently originated loans or loans originated many years ago during their prime educational years.

Figure 3: Percentage of Outstanding Loan Balances that Are Parent PLUS Loans or Other Federal Student Loans, by Age Group, Fiscal Year 2013

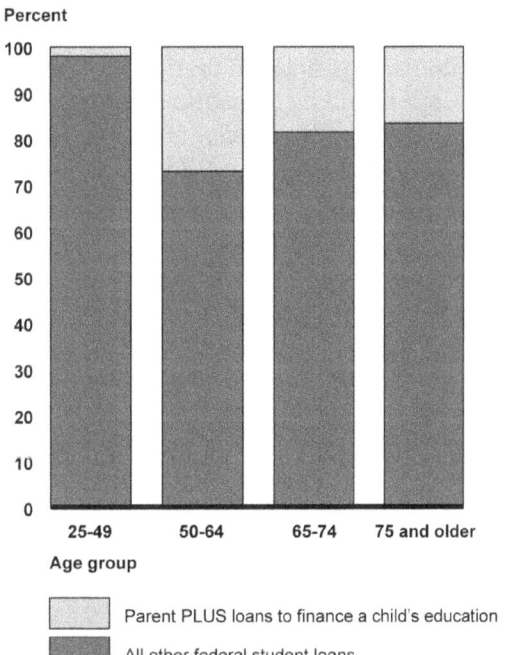

Source: GAO analysis of data provided by the Department of Education. | GAO-14-866T

GAO-14-866T

Older Borrowers Hold Defaulted Federal Student Loans at a Higher Rate and Default Can Have Serious Consequences

Older Borrowers Hold Defaulted Federal Student Loans at a Higher Rate, Especially for Their Own Education

Although older borrowers hold a small portion of federal student loans, they hold defaulted loans at a higher rate than younger borrowers. Individuals 65 or older held 1 percent of outstanding federal student loans in fiscal year 2013 (see fig. 4). However, 12 percent of federal student loans held by individuals age 25 to 49 were in default, while 27 percent of loans held by individuals 65 to 74 were in default, and more than half of loans held by individuals 75 or older were in default.[13]

---

[13]We measured the percentage of default by dividing the number of loans in default by the total number of outstanding loans for each age group. This differs from Education's calculation for cohort default rates, which measures the rate of default for a school's borrowers who enter repayment during a given fiscal year. Education officials noted that the two measures are not directly comparable.

Figure 4: Percentage of Federal Student Loans in Default within Age Groups, Fiscal Year 2013

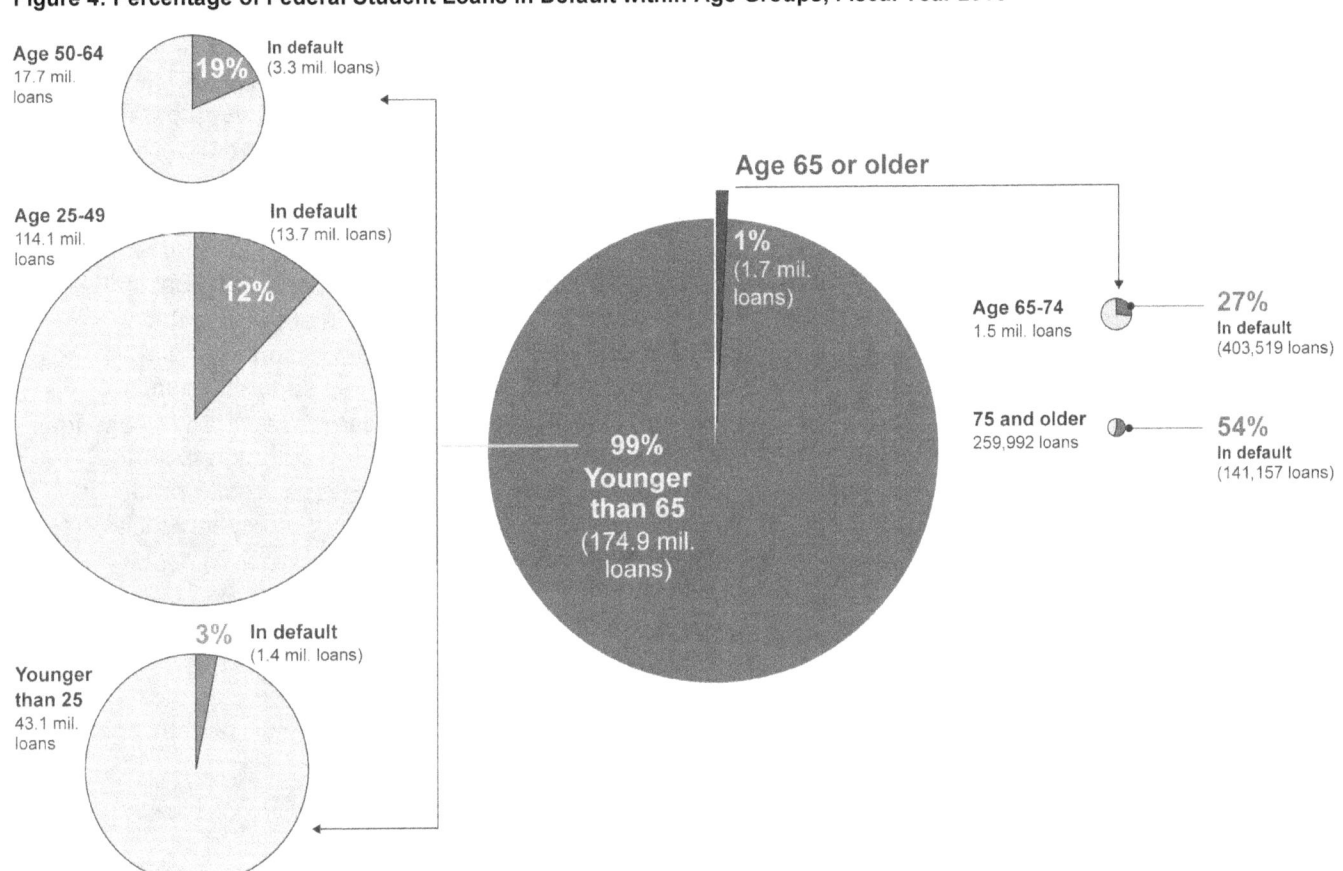

Source: GAO analysis of data from the National Student Loan Data System, Department of Education. | GAO-14-866T

Note: Data is for loans in repayment status as well as loans not in repayment status for reasons such as deferment, forbearance, or a grace period.

According to Education data, older borrowers are in default on federal student loans for their children's education less frequently than they are in default on federal student loans for themselves. Specifically, in fiscal year 2013, 17 percent of Parent PLUS loans held by borrowers ages 65 to 74 were in default, while 30 percent of loans for their own education were in default.

GAO-14-866T

Delinquent Borrowers Have Considerable Time to Begin Repaying Federal Student Loans before Facing Collection Actions, which May Include Withholding Federal Payments

Delinquent borrowers—those who have missed one or more payments—have more than a year to resume payments or negotiate revised terms before facing collection procedures. During the initial year of delinquency for Direct Loans, Education and the loan servicers make a number of attempts to help borrowers arrange for payments and avert default[14] (see fig. 5).[15] After the loan has been delinquent for 425 days (approximately 14 months), Education determines whether to take actions intended to recover the money it is owed. These actions can have serious financial consequences for the borrower. For example, Education may charge collection costs[16] up to 25 percent of the interest and principal of the loan.[17] Interest on the debt continues to accumulate during the delinquency and default period. In addition, Education may garnish wages[18] or initiate litigation. Education may also send the loan to a collection agency. The defaulted debt may also be reported to consumer reporting agencies,[19] which can result in lower credit ratings for the borrower. Lower credit ratings may affect access to credit or rental property, increase interest rates on credit, affect employers' decisions to hire, or increase insurance costs in some states.

---

[14]Default generally occurs when a borrower fails to make a payment for more than 270 days; 20 U.S.C. § 1085(*l*); 34 C.F.R. § 682.200(b). However, Education generally identifies defaulted loans as those 360 days or more past due, because the agency allows loan servicers 90 days to transfer Direct Loans to Education and Federal Family Education Loan lenders up to 90 days to file a default claim with the guarantor.

[15]Outstanding loans made under the Federal Family Education Loan program, also known as guaranteed loans, follow a similar timeline except that defaulted loans are turned over to state guaranty agencies for debt collection, rather than to Education.

[16]34 C.F.R. § 30.60(a)(7).

[17]In re Evans, 322 B.R. 429, 436.

[18]34 C.F.R. § 34.18.

[19]34 C.F.R. § 30.35. Education also reports the borrower's delinquency status to credit bureaus during the life of the loan.

Figure 5: Department of Education Timeline for Delinquent and Defaulted Direct Student Loan Processing

Day 241 — Servicers are required to send the final demand letter, informing the borrower that default will be reported to a credit bureau.

Days in delinquency

Education's loan servicers			Education	
16-180 days	**181-270 days**	**270-360 days**	**At 360 days**	**At 425 days**
Loan servicers must make diligent efforts to contact borrowers at least 4 times by phone and 4 times by mail. Letters must include information on deferment, forbearance, income-sensitive repayment, and other available options to avoid default.	If telephone information is not available, servicers are not required to make further telephone contact.	**Technical default:** Servicers have 90 days to help the borrower to bring the loan current or obtain forbearance or deferment of the loan.	**Default:** Debt is transferred from the servicer to Education, which sends a "welcome letter," informing borrower they have 60 days to pay the loan in full, arrange to pay and make first payment, or to request administrative review. The borrower is no longer eligible for income-based repayment.	Education may: ■ report default to credit agency ■ initiate the process to send the debt to Treasury for offset ■ charge collection fees up to 25 percent of interest and principal ■ initiate administrative wage garnishment ■ initiate litigation ■ send the loan to a collection agency which may: – explain rehabilitation – offer compromise

Source: Department of Education. | GAO-14-866T

At 425 days, Education may also begin the process to send newly defaulted loans to Treasury to recover the debt by withholding a portion of federal payments—known as offset.[20] Federal payments subject to offset include wages for federal employees,[21] tax refunds,[22] and certain monthly federal benefits, such as Social Security retirement and disability payments.[23] Each year, Education prepares a list of newly defaulted loans for Treasury offset. In 2014, newly defaulted debt must have been more than 425 days delinquent before the July deadline so that it can be sent to Treasury in December. If the debt becomes 425 days delinquent after the

---

[20] 34 C.F.R. § 30.20.

[21] 34 C.F.R. pts. 31 and 32.

[22] 31 U.S.C. § 3720A.

[23] 31 U.S.C. § 3716(c)(3)(A). The Debt Collection Improvement Act of 1996 centralized the collection of nontax debt at Treasury. Pub. L. No. 104-134, § 31001, 110 Stat. 1321, 1321-358. The Treasury Offset Program within the Bureau of the Fiscal Service carries out offset of federal payments for nontax debt, including defaulted federal student loans. Offset for student loan debt began in 1999.

cutoff, it would be sent the following December (2015). Thus, the defaulted debt is sent to Treasury 3 to 15 months after 425 days of delinquency—between 17 and 29 months from the last date of payment on the loan (see fig. 6). According to Education officials, loans that have not been paid off are annually recertified as being eligible for offset.

Figure 6: Department of Education's Schedule for Preparing Newly Defaulted Loan Debt for Treasury Offset, 2014

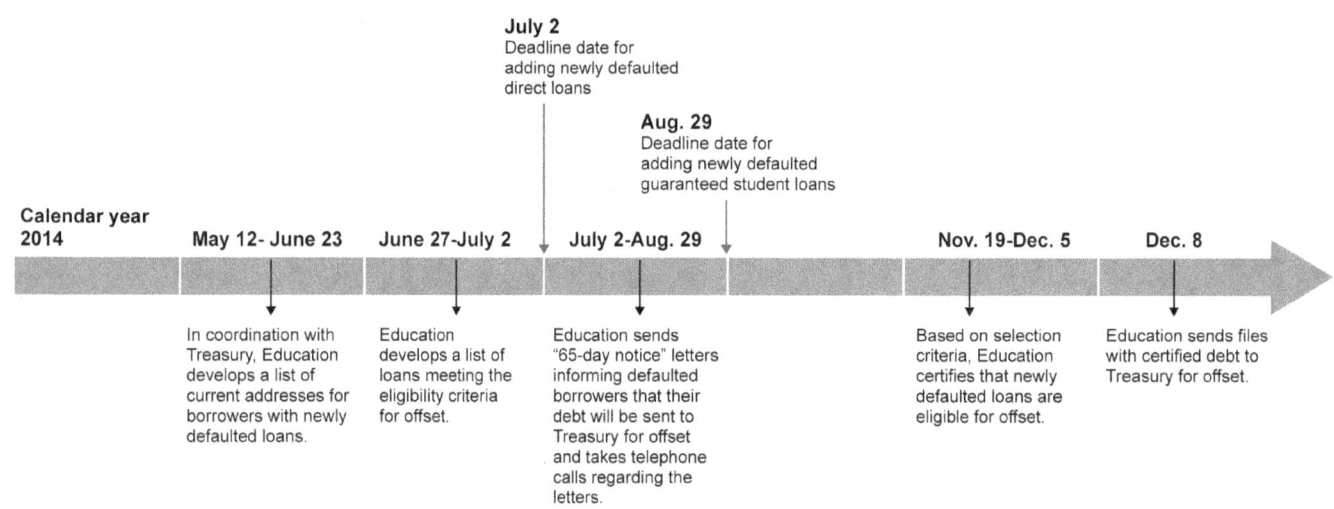

Source: Department of Education. | GAO-14-866T

Note: Certain defaulted debt is not eligible for offset, such as debt being evaluated for discharge, in litigation, or where a Treasury offset hearing has been requested.

After a defaulted loan is certified as eligible for offset to Treasury, certain payments, such as any available tax refunds, are offset immediately, without prior notice to the debtor. Borrowers with monthly benefits available for offset are informed by mail that their benefits will be offset in 60 days and again 30 days before the offset is taken, allowing borrowers an additional 2 months to resume payment on their loan before offset occurs. Treasury assesses a fee[24] for each offset transaction, which is subtracted from the offset payment. Other federal agencies may charge additional fees for each transaction depending on the type of payment being offset. For fiscal year 2014, Treasury's fee was $15 per offset and other agency fees were up to $27.

---

[24]31 U.S.C. § 3716(c)(4).

Federal tax refunds are the source for more than 90 percent of offset collection for federal student loan debt. Offsets from Social Security benefits represented roughly $150 million in 2013 or less than 7 percent of the more than $2.2 billion in federal payments offset by Treasury.

Table 3: Sources of Offset Payments for Federal Student Loan Debt in 2013

Source of Payment	Amount (millions)	Percent of Total
Federal tax refunds	$2,050	91.7
Social Security benefits	$150	6.7
Other	$35	1.6
Total	**$2,235**	**100**

Source: GAO analysis of Department of the Treasury data. | GAO-14-866T

Note: Sources of payment categorized as "Other" include federal salary payments and federal vendor payments.

The number of borrowers, especially older borrowers, who have experienced offsets to Social Security retirement, survivor, or disability benefits to repay defaulted federal student loans has increased over time.[25] In 2002, the first full year during which Social Security benefits were offset by Treasury, about 31,000 borrowers were affected.[26] Of those borrowers, about 19 percent (6,000) were 65 or older. From 2002 through 2013, the number of borrowers whose Social Security benefits were offset has increased roughly 400 percent, and the number of borrowers 65 and over increased roughly 500 percent (see fig. 7). In

---

[25]Specifically, the Social Security benefits that Treasury offsets are Federal Old-Age, Survivors, and Disability Insurance Benefits, issued under Title II of the Social Security Act. Treasury does not differentiate among retirement, survivor, and disability benefits in administering Social Security benefit offsets, since all of these benefits are eligible for offset. Supplemental Security Income benefits have been exempted from offset.

[26]The Debt Collection Improvement Act of 1996 necessitated Treasury promulgate (in consultation with the Social Security Administration, Railroad Retirement Board, Department of Labor, Department of Veterans Affairs, Office of Management and Budget, and others) regulations before it offset any Social Security benefits, and those regulations were finalized on December 23, 1998. Offset of Federal Benefit Payments to Collect Past-due, Legally Enforceable Nontax Debt, 63 Fed. Reg. 44,986 (Aug. 21, 1998) (interim rule with request for comments) and 63 Fed. Reg. 71,204 (final rule). Treasury officials said that Treasury had to develop a system to process Social Security benefit offsets, including developing a way to provide information on offsets back to the Social Security Administration, before beginning offset of Social Security benefits in mid-2001.

2013, Social Security benefits for about 155,000 people were offset and about 36,000 of those were 65 and over.[27]

Figure 7: Number of Federal Student Loan Borrowers Whose Social Security Retirement, Survivor, or Disability Benefits Were Offset, By Age, 2002-2013

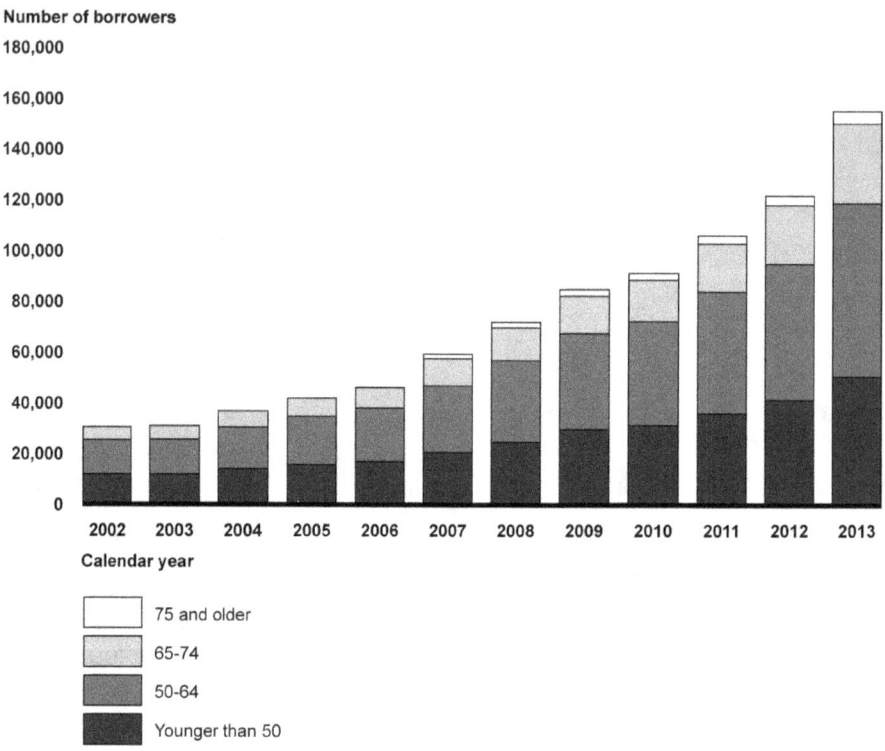

Source: GAO analysis of Treasury and Social Security Administration data. | GAO-14-866T

The majority of Social Security benefit offsets for federal student loan debt are from disability benefits rather than retirement or survivor

---

[27]While defaulted federal student loan debt can lead to reduced Social Security benefits once in retirement, the presence of student loan debt for those nearing retirement can also affect retirement security as it may keep individuals from saving for retirement.

benefits.[28] In 2013, 70.6 percent of defaulted borrowers (105,000) whose Social Security benefits were offset received disability benefits (see fig. 8).[29] That year, about $97 million was collected through offset from disability benefits. For borrowers 65 and over, the majority of Social Security offsets are from retirement and survivor benefits because Social Security disability benefits automatically convert to retirement benefits at the beneficiary's full retirement age, currently 66.[30] About 33,000 borrowers age 65 and over had Social Security retirement or survivor benefits offset in 2013 to repay defaulted federal student loans.

Figure 8: Federal Student Loan Borrowers with Social Security Benefit Offsets in 2013, By Age of Borrower and Type of Benefit

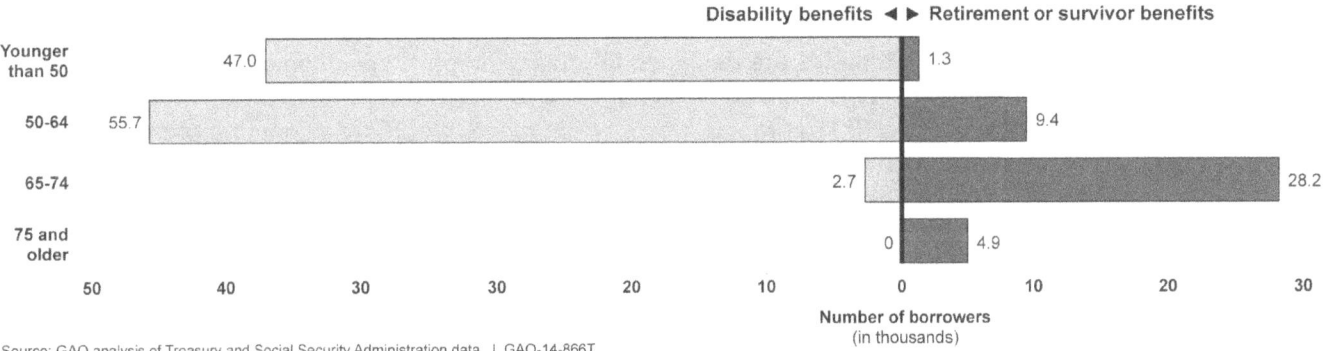

Source: GAO analysis of Treasury and Social Security Administration data. | GAO-14-866T

Note: The Social Security Administration automatically converts disability benefits to retirement benefits at the beneficiary's full retirement age, currently age 66. 20 C.F.R. § 404.316(b)(2).

---

[28]Borrowers with a total and permanent disability may apply for discharge of their federal student loans by providing, for example, a notice of award for Social Security Disability Insurance benefits indicating that the borrower's next scheduled disability review will be within five to seven years. 20 U.S.C. § 1087(a)(1), 34 C.F.R. §§ 674.61(b)(2)(iv)(B) and 682.402(c)(2)(iv)(B). Between July 1, 2013 and May 31, 2014, Education received 196,851 *applications for disability discharges and approved 139,855 in the same period. Education informs borrowers about disability discharge during mandatory loan entrance and exit counseling, and borrowers can learn about disability discharge through Education's websites or by contacting their loan servicer.*

[29]For less than 5 percent of Social Security benefit offset payments, we were unable to determine whether the offset was taken from a disability insurance payment or we were unable to determine the age of the borrower. We excluded these payments from our analysis.

[30] 20 C.F.R. § 404.316(b)(2).

The amount of money collected from Social Security benefit offsets to repay defaulted federal student loans has also increased, but the average amount offset on a monthly basis per borrower has remained relatively stable. Treasury collected about $24 million in offsets from Social Security benefits in 2002, about $108 million in 2012, and about $150 million in 2013. However, over this period, the average amount offset on a monthly basis per borrower rose only slightly, from around $120 in the early 2000s to a little over $130 in 2013.

Adjusting Current Limits for Offset Can Keep Monthly Benefits Above the Poverty Threshold, but Reduce Collections to Pay Defaulted Federal Student Loans

Although there are statutory limits under the Debt Collection Improvement Act of 1996 (DCIA)[31] on the amount that Treasury can offset from monthly federal benefits, the current limits may result in monthly benefits below the poverty threshold for certain defaulted borrowers. Social Security benefits are designed to replace, in part, the income lost due to retirement, disability, or death of the worker.[32] The DCIA set a level of $750 per month below which monthly benefits cannot be offset. In 1998, the amount of allowable offset was effectively modified under regulations, to the lesser of 15 percent of the total benefit or the amount by which the benefit exceeds $750 per month, thus creating a standard more favorable to defaulted borrowers.[33] For example, a borrower with a Social Security benefit of $1,000 per month would have an offset of $150, because that is the lesser of 15 percent of the benefit—$150—and the amount of the benefit over $750, which is $250. This offset would leave the borrower with a monthly benefit of $850, which is below the poverty threshold for 2013. The statutory limit of $750 for an offset was above the poverty threshold when it was set, in 1998. The offset limits have not changed since 1998, and the $750 limit represented about 81 percent of the poverty threshold for a single adult 65 and over in 2013. If the $750 limit had been indexed to the changes in the poverty threshold since 1998, in 2013 it would have increased by 43 percent or to about $1,073 (see fig. 9). Borrowers with benefits below this amount would not have been offset.

---

[31]Pub. L. No. 104-134, § 31001(d)(2)(D), § 3716(c)(3)(A)(ii), 110 Stat. 1321, 1321-360 (codified at 31 U.S.C. § 3716(c)(3)(A)(ii)).

[32]In 2011, more than a third of beneficiaries 65 and over relied on Social Security benefits for 90 percent or more of their income.

[33]Offset should not exceed the amount of the debt. 31 C.F.R. § 285.4(e).

GAO-14-866T

Figure 9: Comparison of Offset Limit if Indexed to Poverty Threshold

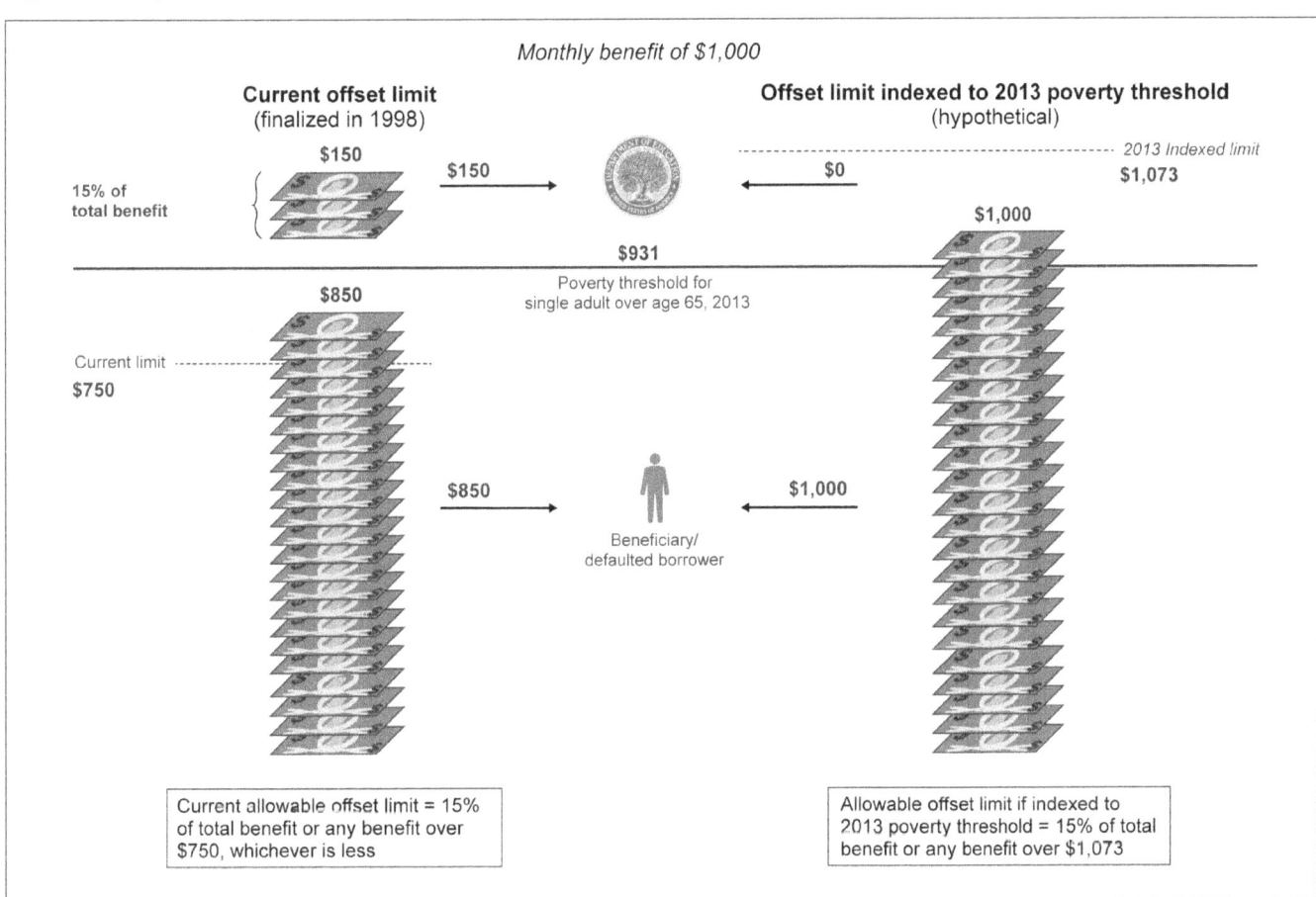

Source: GAO analysis based on relevant laws and regulation. | GAO-14-866T

Indexing monthly benefit offset limits to the poverty threshold can prevent some older borrowers from having offsets, but would also reduce Education's recoveries from Social Security offsets. If the offset limit had been indexed to match the rate of increase in the poverty threshold, in 2013, 68 percent of all borrowers whose Social Security benefits were offset for federal student loan debt would have kept their entire benefit, including 61 percent of borrowers 65 and older. An additional 15 percent of all borrowers and borrowers age 65 and older would have kept more of their benefits in that year. However, indexing the offset limit would have reduced the amount collected from Social Security benefits by approximately 60 percent or $94 million in 2013, representing about 4.2

percent of all dollars offset from all sources by Treasury for student loan debt in that year.

In conclusion, student loan debt and default are problems for a small percentage of older Americans. As the amount of student loan debt held by Americans age 65 and older increases, the prospect of default implies greater financial risk for those at or near retirement—especially for those dependent on Social Security. Most of the federal student loan debt held by older Americans was obtained for their own education, suggesting that it may have been held for an extended period, accumulating interest over time. The Social Security retirement or survivor benefits of about 33,000 Americans age 65 and older were reduced through offset to meet defaulted federal student loan obligations in 2013. Because the statutory limit at which monthly benefits can be offset has not been updated since it was enacted in 1998, certain defaulted borrowers with offsets are left with Social Security benefits below the poverty threshold. As the baby boomers continue to move into retirement, the number of older Americans with defaulted loans will only continue to increase. This creates the potential for an unpleasant surprise for some, as their benefits are offset and they face the possibility of a less secure retirement.

Chairman Nelson, Ranking Member Collins, and Members of the Committee, this completes my prepared statement. I would be pleased to respond to any questions that you may have at this time.

GAO Contact and Staff Acknowledgments

If you or your staff have any questions about this testimony, please contact me at (202) 512-7215 or jeszeckc@gao.gov. Contact points for our Offices of Congressional Relations and Public Affairs may be found on the last page of this statement. GAO staff who made key contributions to this testimony are listed in appendix II.

Appendix I: Objectives, Scope, and Methodology

To understand the extent to which older Americans have outstanding student loans and how this debt compares to other types of debt, we relied primarily on data from the Federal Reserve Board's Survey of Consumer Finances (SCF), a survey that is conducted once every 3 years and gathers detailed information on the finances of U.S. families.[1] SCF data is publicly available and was extracted from the Federal Reserve Board's website.[2] Specifically, we analyzed data from the 2004, 2007, and 2010 SCF to provide a range of information, including an overview of the percentage of families, by age of head of household, with student debt over time. An important limitation of the data is that debt, including student loans, is reported at the household level. As a result, the SCF survey responses represent the debt of the entire household, not just the head of household. Therefore, it is possible that for some households headed by older Americans, the reported student debt is actually held by children or other dependents that are still members of the household, rather than the older head of household.

In addition, to describe the trend in federal student loan balances among older Americans and approximate the loans older Americans had taken for themselves or for their children, we obtained data from the Department of Education's National Student Loan Data System (NSLDS).[3] Specifically, we used data from summary tables that Education provided containing data from NSLDS for fiscal years 2005 through 2013. We assessed the reliability of this data by reviewing data documentation and the queries used to create the summary tables from the underlying data system and by interviewing technical staff at Education involved in creating the summary tables. We determined that the data elements we used were sufficiently reliable for the purposes of

---

[1]To ensure representativeness of the survey, respondents are selected at random and the survey seeks to select families from all economic strata. In addition to education loans, the 2010 SCF inquired about financial assets, income and taxes, businesses, vehicles, credit attitudes and credit cards, and other matters.

[2]The 2010 SCF did not use the phrase "student loans," but rather asked respondents whether they have loans for educational expenses. However, for consistency in usage, we will use the phrases "student loans" or "student loan debt" throughout this report. Because of the inclusive wording of the question, the SCF data reflects both federal and private loans.

[3]The NSLDS is a comprehensive national database maintained by the Department of Education that is used to readily access student aid data and track money appropriated as aid for postsecondary students. The database includes data on the various federal student loan programs.

this testimony. The NSLDS data we obtained allows us to count federal
student loans and loan balances, but not the number of borrowers.
Although Education maintains borrower-level data, we were only able to
obtain aggregated data by loan type during the course of our analyses.
These summary tables reported that about 1,000 of the more than 6
million Parent PLUS loans outstanding in fiscal year 2013 were to
borrowers under the age of 25. According to Education, these cases
resulted from a reporting issue where the date of birth of the Parent PLUS
borrower was the reported as being the same as that of the student. We
excluded these Parent PLUS loans from our analysis.

To understand the extent to which older Americans defaulted on federal
student loans and the possible consequences of such a default, we relied
on a number of data sources and agency documents related to federal
student loans. To determine the extent to which older Americans have
defaulted on federal student loans, we used data from the NSLDS
summary tables we received from Education. To evaluate the
consequences of default, we reviewed federal law, regulations, and
agency documents describing the collection process for defaulted federal
student loans, including offset of federal benefit payments through the
Treasury Offset Program (TOP). We interviewed officials at Education
involved in managing defaulted federal student loans, and we interviewed
officials at Treasury, Education, and the Social Security Administration
about the process for offsetting Social Security retirement, survivor, and
disability benefits through the TOP. In addition, we interviewed Education
officials and reviewed relevant documentation regarding Education's debt
collection policies and procedures; however, we did not audit their
compliance with statutory requirements related to these activities.

To describe the extent of Treasury offset of Social Security Administration
benefits for federal student loan debt, we used data on offset payments
from the TOP for fiscal years 2001 through 2014. We assessed the
reliability of this data by reviewing data documentation, conducting
electronic testing on the data, and interviewing Treasury staff about the
reliability of this data. Because the TOP data does not include the age of
borrowers or the type of Social Security benefits that were offset, we
obtained such information for relevant borrowers from the Social Security
Administration's Master Beneficiary Record using a match on Social
Security numbers. We assessed the reliability of the data by reviewing
data documentation, obtaining the computer code used to match
borrowers to the Master Beneficiary Record, and interviewing the staff at
the Social Security Administration who conducted the match. We
determined that the data elements we used were sufficiently reliable for

the purposes of this testimony. For about 0.25 percent of borrowers, we were unable to determine the borrower's age, and we excluded these borrowers from age-based analyses. For about 4.3 percent of offset payments, we were unable to determine the type of benefit, and we excluded these payments from the analysis of the type of benefit that was offset. To evaluate the extent to which Social Security benefits would have been offset if the $750 limit below which benefits are not offset had been adjusted for changes in the poverty threshold, we analyzed TOP data to impute the amount of a monthly Social Security benefit payment from the size of the offset that was taken from that payment. We then applied a modified set of rules for calculating an offset amount to the imputed benefit, changing the $750 limit to $1,072.50—the adjusted amount for the limit had it been indexed to the poverty threshold—to estimate, for 2013, whether the monthly benefit payment would have been offset had the offset limit increased at the rate of the poverty threshold.

Appendix II: GAO Contacts and Staff Acknowledgments

GAO Contact	Charles A. Jeszeck, Director, (202) 512-7215 or jeszeckc@gao.gov
Staff Acknowledgments	In addition to the contact named above, Michael Collins (Assistant Director), Michael Hartnett, Margaret Weber, Christopher Zbrozek, and Lacy Vong made key contributions to this testimony. In addition, key support was provided by Ben Bolitzer, Ying Long, John Mingus, Mimi Nguyen, Kathleen van Gelder, Walter Vance, and Craig Winslow.

www.ingramcontent.com/pod-product-compliance
Lightning Source LLC
Chambersburg PA
CBHW080754290526
45790CB00008B/3437